COLOR, CUT, AND FOLD
CHRISTMAS ORNAMENTS

Skyhorse Publishing books may be purchased in bulk at special discounts for sales promotion, corporate gifts, fund-raising, or educational purposes. Special editions can also be created to specifications. For details, contact the Special Sales Department, Skyhorse Publishing, 307 West 36th Street, 11th Floor, New York, NY 10018 or info@skyhorsepublishing.com.

Skyhorse® and Skyhorse Publishing® are registered trademarks of Skyhorse Publishing, Inc.®, a Delaware corporation.

Visit our website at www.skyhorsepublishing.com.

10 9 8 7 6 5 4 3 2

Cover design by Brian Peterson
Cover photography by Allan Penn

Print ISBN: 978-1-5107-1421-2

Printed in the United States of America

COLOR, CUT, AND FOLD
CHRISTMAS ORNAMENTS

30 EASY, CREATIVE PROJECTS FOR THE HOLIDAYS

ILLUSTRATIONS BY AMANDA BRACK

Skyhorse Publishing

Fold Your Own Beautiful Ornaments

Make the season bright with *Color, Cut, and Fold Christmas Ornaments*! These one-of-a-kind holiday ornaments are easy to color in, cut out, and fold into three-dimensional decorations for your home, tree, or for giving as fun gifts. Get together with friends and family for holiday crafting, or make these on your own to bring splendor to the season!

This book features thirty completely unique, hand-drawn designs on three different ornament templates. Color in the lines, then follow the key and simple instructions to cut and fold the ornaments into 3-D decorations. Tuck a loop of festive ribbon inside the ornaments as you put them together, or simply attach a hook to the top of each finished orb or star for hanging. Immerse yourself in the relaxing activity of coloring while you make something beautiful! Decorate these gorgeously illustrated ornaments for your themed holiday parties, festive occasions, or just for fun!

How to Make Your Ornaments

The distinct lines on the ornaments indicate where to cut, fold, and glue:
- CUT solid black lines.
- FOLD dotted gray lines.
- APPLY GLUE or DOUBLE-SIDED TAPE to solid gray tabs and adhere to the shape directly to the right.

Circle Ornament
1. With a penknife or scissors, carefully cut out all four circles along the black lines.
2. Fold each circle down the middle along the gray-dotted lines. The design will fold inward.
3. Apply glue or double-sided tape to the reverse side of each circle.
4. Attach the folded segment of one circle to a corresponding folded segment of another circle. Repeat until you have a three-dimensional orb with four faces.
   Remember: Place a hook or looped ribbon in the center of the ornament as you form the shape.

Lantern Ornament
1. With a penknife or scissors, carefully cut out all four lanterns along the black lines.
2. Fold each gray tab along gray-dotted lines. The tabs will fold behind the shape.
3. Apply glue or double-sided tape to each gray tab.
4. Attach the folded tabs of each lantern segment to the back of the lantern segment directly to the right. When finished, you will have a three-dimensional lantern with three faces.
   Remember: Place a hook or looped ribbon in the center of the ornament as you form the shape.

Star Ornament
1. With a penknife or scissors, carefully cut out both stars along the black lines.
2. Fold each section of the star along the gray-dotted lines in alternating creases: the long points will fold outward, but the inner corners will fold inward. (This will cause the long points and center of the star to pop outward when the ornament is complete.)
3. Fold each gray tab along gray-dotted lines. The tabs will fold behind the shape.
4. Apply glue or double-sided tape to each gray tab.
5. Attach the folded tabs of each star point to the back of the other cut-out's star points. (Essentially, the cut-outs will be back-to-back.) When finished, you will have a three-dimensional star with two faces.
   Remember: Place a hook or looped ribbon in the center of the ornament as you form the shape.

Cut

Glue/Tape

Fold

Cut

Glue/Tape

Fold

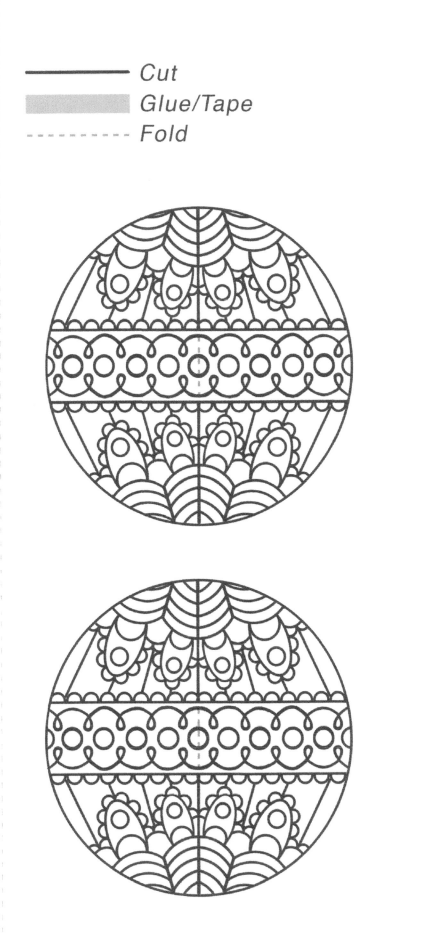

Cut

Glue/Tape

Fold

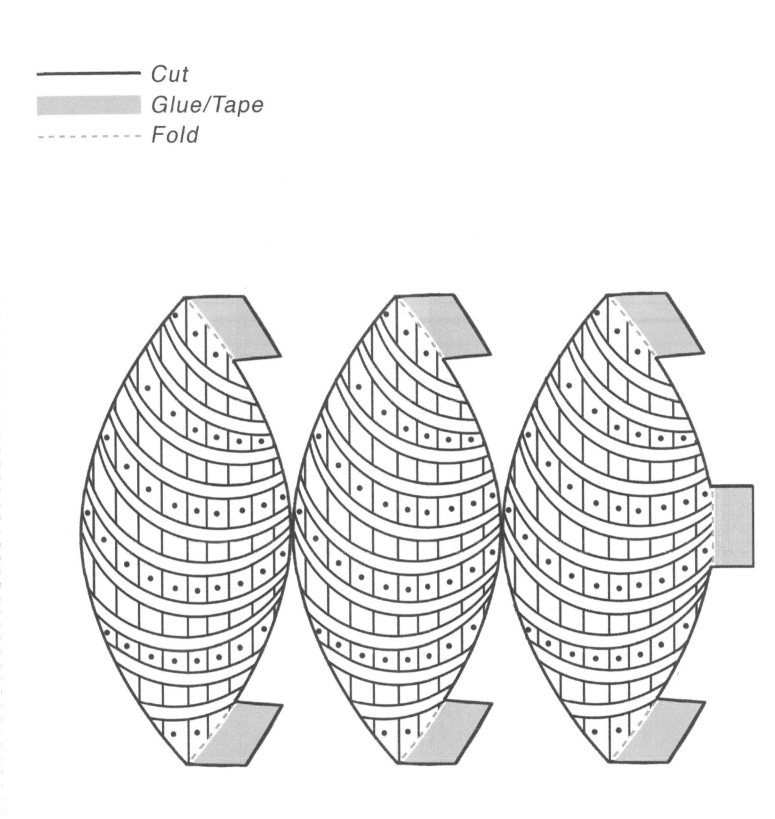

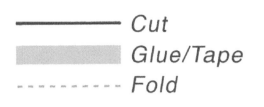

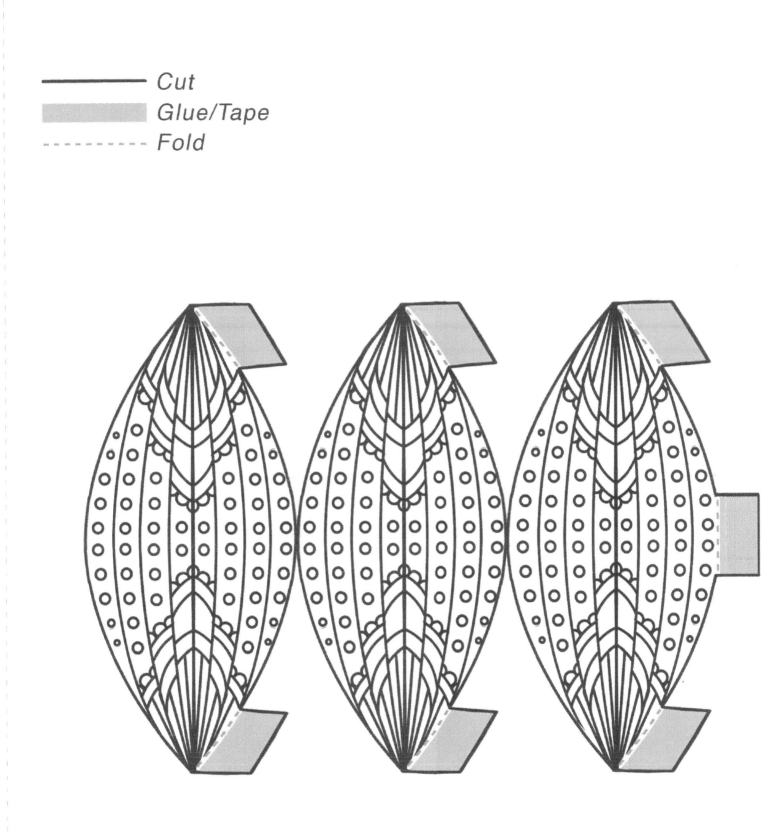

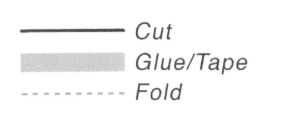

Cut

Glue/Tape

Fold

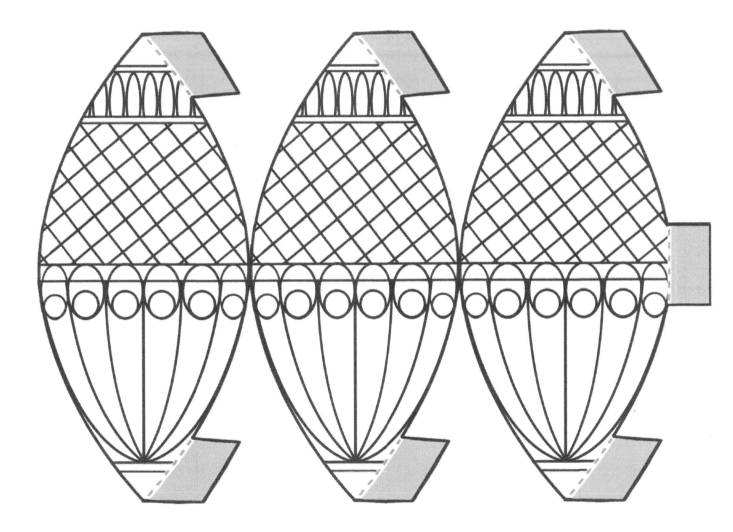

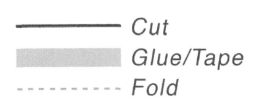
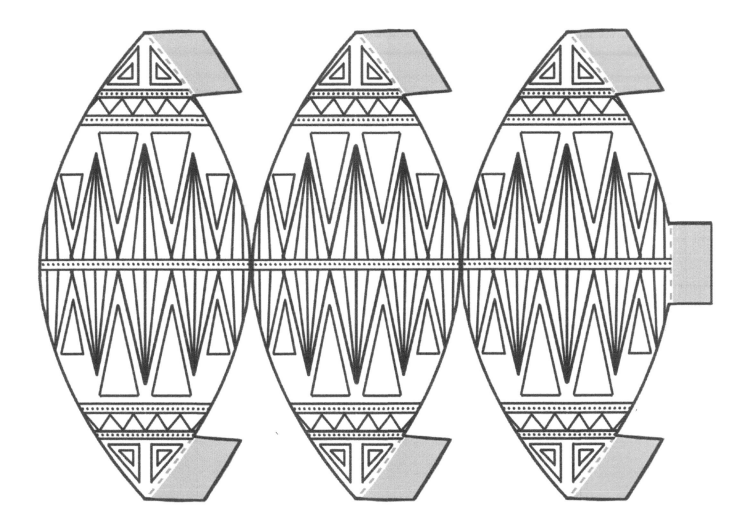

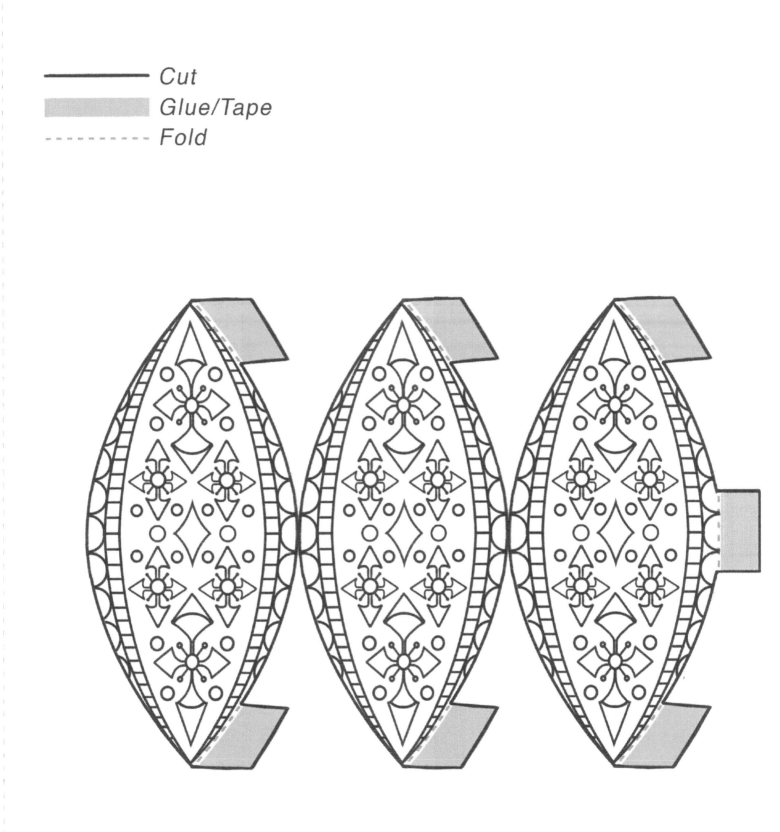

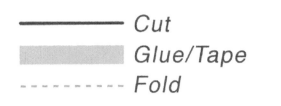

Cut

Glue/Tape

Fold

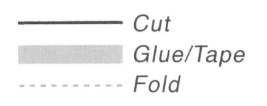
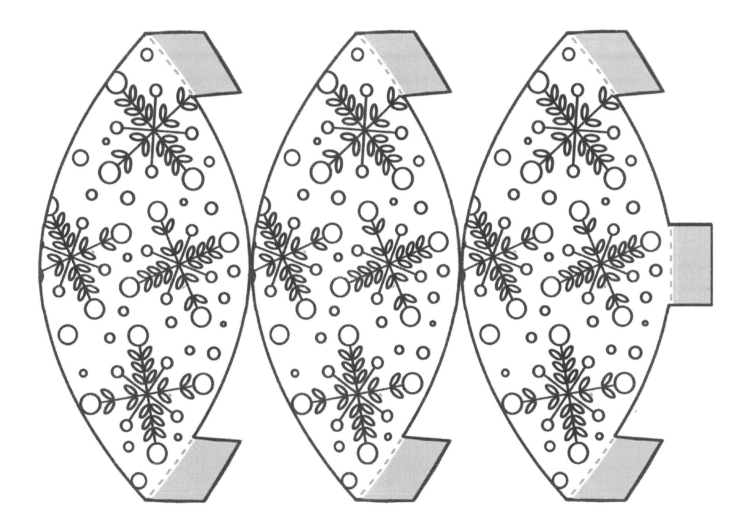

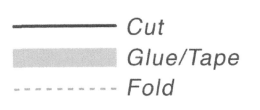

Cut
Glue/Tape
Fold

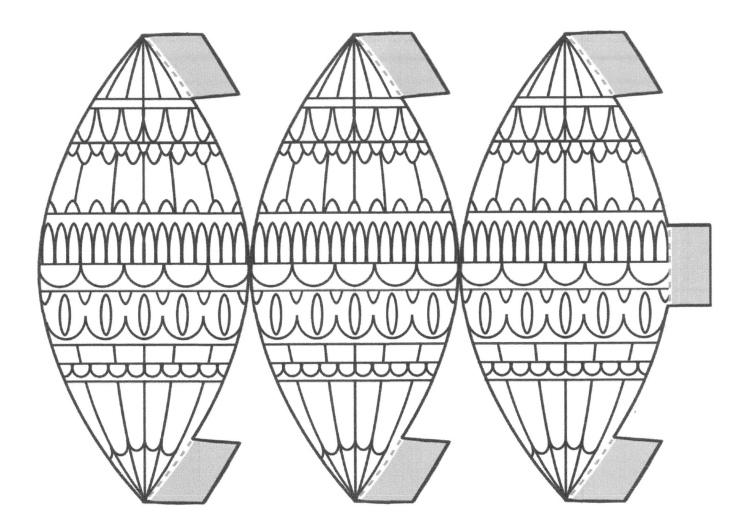

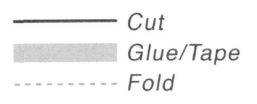

Cut

Glue/Tape

Fold

Cut

Glue/Tape

Fold

Cut

Glue/Tape

Fold

Cut

Glue/Tape

Fold

Cut

Glue/Tape

Fold

a

avianne

Cut

Glue/Tape

Fold

Cut
Glue/Tape
Fold

Cut

Glue/Tape

Fold